William Sinclair Lord

The Best Short Poems of the 19th Century

William Sinclair Lord

The Best Short Poems of the 19th Century

ISBN/EAN: 9783337006204

Printed in Europe, USA, Canada, Australia, Japan

Cover: Foto ©Thomas Meinert / pixelio.de

More available books at **www.hansebooks.com**

The Best Short Poems of
The Nineteenth Century

BEING THE TWENTY-FIVE BEST
SHORT POEMS AS SELECTED BY
BALLOT BY COMPETENT CRITICS

COMPILED BY

WILLIAM S. LORD

Author of "Blue and Gold," "Jingle and Jangle," etc.

Fleming H. Revell Company

Chicago : New York : Toronto

1899

NOTE.

TWO hundred representative literary people were recently asked for a list of "twenty-five of the best short poems (limit fifty lines) written in the English language in the nineteenth century." This request met with a ready response. Lists were received from prominent poets, critics, editors, educators, and others interested in poetry. These lists were carefully prepared. The names of those who so kindly gave valuable time and study in preparing them would be given had not the request been made, in a number of instances, that the list submitted be considered confidential. This emphasizes the value of the verdict as being a perfectly free expression of the minds best qualified to judge of the merits of the poetry of the period.

No individual list is given. The twenty-five poems which received the highest number of votes will, it is hoped, make an acceptable "nut-shell anthology." They are arranged in order according to the ballots cast, "The Chambered Nautilus," which received the highest vote, being number one on the list.

A supplementary list of two hundred poems is arranged alphabetically by authors. These poems received votes, but none received enough to place it among the first twenty-five.

It is, perhaps, worthy of note that when these lists were prepared Mr. Kipling had not written "Recessional," which would undoubtedly, at this time, be placed well among the first.

The names of Lowell, Longfellow and Whittier do

not appear, while Bryant is represented by "To a
Waterfowl," and not by "Thanatopsis." America's
bards number five, while Tennyson's name appears
four times and Wordsworth's name three times.

In the supplementary list Longfellow is represented
by nine titles, Lowell by ten, Tennyson by fifteen,
Wordsworth by six and Whittier by five.

Dr. Holmes's "Chambered Nautilus," Mrs. Howe's
"Battle-Hymn of the Republic," and "Emerson's
"Concord Fight" are published by permission of
Messrs. Houghton, Mifflin & Co., the publishers of
the works of Emerson and Holmes and of Mrs.
Howe's poems. "Crossing the Bar" is reprinted from
The Macmillan Company's complete edition of Lord
Tennyson's poems.

W. S. L.

March, 1899, Evanston, Ill.

THE BEST SHORT POEMS OF THE NINETEENTH CENTURY

The Best Short Poems

OF THE

Nineteenth Century.

❧❧

I.

THE CHAMBERED NAUTILUS.*

THIS is the ship of pearl, which, poets feign,
    Sails the unshadowed main,—
    The venturous bark that flings
On the sweet summer wind its purple wings
In gulfs enchanted, where the Siren sings,
    And coral reefs lie bare,
Where the cold sea-maids rise to sun their streaming
hair.

Its webs of living gauze no more unfurl;
    Wrecked is the ship of pearl!
    And every chambered cell,
Where its dim dreaming life was wont to dwell,
As the frail tenant shaped his growing shell,
    Before thee lies revealed,—
Its irised ceiling rent, its sunless crypt unsealed!

Year after year beheld the silent toil
    That spread his lustrous coil;
    Still, as the spiral grew,
He left the past year's dwelling for the new,
Stole with soft step its shining arch-way through,
    Built up its idle door,
Stretched in his last-found home, and knew the old no
more.

Thanks for the heavenly message brought by thee,
    Child of the wandering sea,
    Cast from her lap, forlorn!
From thy dead lips a clearer note is born
Than ever Triton blew from wreathed horn!
    While on my ear it rings,
Through the deep caves of thought I hear a voice that
sings:—

Build thee more stately mansions, O my soul,
    As the swift seasons roll!
    Leave thy low-vaulted past!
Let each new temple, nobler than the last,
Shut thee from heaven with a dome more vast,
    Till thou at length art free,
Leaving thine outgrown shell by life's unresting sea!
                —*Oliver Wendell Holmes.*
                    1809-1894.

II.

BUGLE SONG.

THE splendor falls on castle walls
　　And snowy summits old in story;
The long light shakes across the lakes,
　　And the wild cataract leaps in glory.
Blow, bugle, blow, set the wild echoes flying,
Blow, bugle; answer, echoes, dying, dying, dying.

　　O hark, O hear! how thin and clear,
　　　　And thinner, clearer, farther going!
　　O sweet and far, from cliff and scar,
　　　　The horns of Elfland faintly blowing!
Blow, let us hear the purple glens replying:
Blow, bugle; answer, echoes, dying, dying, dying.

　　O love, they die in yon rich sky,
　　　　They faint on hill or field or river:
　　Our echoes roll from soul to soul,
　　　　Which grow forever and forever.
Blow, bugle, blow, set the wild echoes flying,
And answer, echoes, answer, dying, dying, dying.
　　　　　　　　　—Alfred, Lord Tennyson.
　　　　　　　　　　　1809-1892.

III.

CROSSING THE BAR.

SUNSET and evening star,
    And one clear call for me!
And may there be no moaning of the bar
    When I put out to sea,

But such a tide as moving seems asleep,
    Too full for sound and foam,
When that which drew from out the boundless deep
    Turns again home.

Twilight and evening bell,
    And after that the dark!
And may there be no moaning of farewell,
    When I embark.

For though from out our bourne of time and place
    The flood may bear me far,
I hope to see my Pilot face to face
    When I have crossed the bar.

—Alfred, Lord Tennyson,
1809-1892.

IV.

BATTLE-HYMN OF THE REPUBLIC.*

MINE eyes have seen the glory of the coming of
the Lord;
He is tramping out the vintage where the grapes of
wrath are stored!
He hath loosed the fateful lightning of his terrible
swift sword;
His truth is marching on.

I have seen him in the watch-fires of a hundred cir-
cling camps;
They have builded him an altar in the evening dews
and damps:
I have read his righteous sentence by the dim and
flaring lamps:
His day is marching on.

I have read a fiery gospel writ in burnished rows of
steel:
"As ye deal with my contemners, so with you my
grace shall deal:
Let the Hero, born of woman, crush the serpent with
his heel,
Since God is marching on."

He has sounded forth the trumpet that shall never call
    retreat;
He is sifting out the hearts of men before his judg-
    ment seat;
O, be swift, my soul, to answer him! be jubilant, my
    feet!
      Our God is marching on.

In the beauty of the lilies Christ was born across the
    sea,
With a glory in his bosom that transfigures you and
    me:
As he died to make men holy, let us die to make men
    free,
      While God is marching on.

—Julia Ward Howe.
1819 ——

V.

THE LOST LEADER.

JUST for a handful of silver he left us,
   Just for a ribbon to stick in his coat—
Found the one gift of which fortune bereft us,
   Lost all the others she lets us devote;
They, with the gold to give, dol'd him out silver,
   So much was theirs who so little allow'd;
How all our copper had gone for his service!
   Rags—were they purple, his heart had been proud!
We that had lov'd him so, follow'd him, honor'd him,
   Liv'd in his mild and magnificent eye,
Learn'd his great language, caught his clear accents,
   Made him our pattern to live and to die!
Shakespeare was of us, Milton was for us,
   Burns, Shelley, were with us,—they watch from
      their graves!
He alone breaks from the van and the freeman,
   He alone sinks to the rear and the slaves!

We shall march prospering,—not thro' his presence;
   Songs may inspirit us,—not from his lyre;
Deeds will be done,—while he boasts his quiescence,
   Still bidding crouch whom the rest bade aspire.
Blot out his name, then, record one lost soul more,
   One task more declin'd, one more footpath untrod,
One more devil's· triumph and sorrow for angels,
   One wrong more to man, one more insult to God!

Life's night begins: let him never come back to us!
  There would be doubt, hesitation, and pain,
Forced praise on our part—the glimmer of twilight,
  Never glad confident morning again!
Best fight on well, for we taught him—strike gal-
    lantly,
  Menace our heart ere we master his own;
Then let him receive the new knowledge and wait us,
  Pardon'd in heaven, the first by the throne!
                          —*Robert Browning*.
                          1812-1890.

VI.

ON FIRST LOOKING INTO
CHAPMAN'S HOMER.

MUCH have I travell'd in the realms of gold
    And many goodly states and kingdoms seen,
Round many western islands have I been
Which bards in fealty to Apollo hold.

Oft of one wide expanse had I been told
    That deep-brow'd Homer ruled as his demesne:
    Yet did I never breathe its pure serene
Till I heard Chapman speak out loud and bold:

—Then felt I like some watcher of the skies
    When a new planet swims into his ken;
Or like stout Cortez—when with eagle eyes

He stared at the Pacific, and all his men
    Look'd at each other with a wild surmise—
Silent, upon a peak in Darien.

                    —*John Keats.*
                    1795-1821.

VII.

ODE ON A GRECIAN URN

THOU still unravish'd bride of quietness!
    Thou foster child of Silence and slow Time,
Sylvan historian, who canst thus express
A flowery tale more sweetly than our rhyme:
What leaf-fringed legend haunts about thy shape
Of deities or mortals, or of both,
In Tempe or the dales of Arcady?
What men or gods are these? what maidens loath?
What mad pursuit? What struggle to escape?
What pipes and timbrels? What wild ecstasy?

Heard melodies are sweet, but those unheard
Are sweeter; therefore, ye soft pipes, play on;
Not to the sensual ear, but, more endear'd,
Pipe to the spirit ditties of no tone:
Fair youth, beneath the trees, thou canst not leave
Thy song, nor ever can those trees be bare;
Bold Lover, never, never canst thou kiss,
Though winning near the goal—yet, do not grieve;
She cannot fade, though thou hast not thy bliss,
Forever wilt thou love, and she be fair!

Ah, happy, happy boughs! that cannot shed
Your leaves, nor ever bid the Spring adieu;
And, happy melodist, unwearied,
Forever piping songs forever new;
More happy love! more happy, happy love!

Forever warm and still to be enjoy'd,
Forever panting and forever young;
All breathing human passion far above,
That leaves a heart high sorrowful and cloy'd
A burning forehead, and a parching tongue.

Who are these coming to the sacrifice?
To what green altar, O mysterious priest,
Lead'st thou that heifer lowing at the skies,
And all her silken flanks with garlands drest?
What little town by river or sea-shore,
Or mountain-built with peaceful citadel,
Is emptied of its folk, this pious morn?
And, little town, thy streets forevermore
Will silent be; and not a soul to tell
Why thou art desolate, can e'er return.

O Attic shape! Fair attitude! with brede
Of marble men and maidens overwrought,
With forest branches and the trodden weed;
Thou, silent form! dost tease us out of thought
As dost eternity: Cold Pastoral!
When old age shall this generation waste,
Thou shalt remain, in midst of other woe
Than ours, a friend to man, to whom thou say'st,
"Beauty is truth, truth beauty,"—that is all
Ye know on earth, and all ye need to know.
                              —*John Keats.*
                              1795-1821.

VIII.

SHE WAS A PHANTOM OF DELIGHT.

SHE was a Phantom of delight
    When first she gleam'd upon my sight;
A lovely Apparition, sent
To be a moment's ornament;
Her eyes as stars of twilight fair;
Like Twilight's, too, her dusky hair;
But all things else about her drawn
From May-time and the cheerful dawn;
A dancing shape, an image gay,
To haunt, to startle, and waylay.

I saw her upon nearer view,
A Spirit, yet a Woman, too!
Her household motions light and free,
And steps of virgin liberty;
A countenance in which did meet
Sweet records, promises as sweet;
A creature not too bright or good
For human nature's daily food,
For transient sorrows, simple wiles,
Praise, blame, love, kisses, tears, and smiles.

And now I see with eye serene
The very pulse of the machine;
A being breathing thoughtful breath,
A traveler between life and death:
The reason firm, the temperate will,
Endurance, foresight, strength, and skill;
A perfect woman, nobly plann'd
To warn, to comfort, and command;
And yet a Spirit still, and bright
With something of an angel-light.
                —*William Wordsworth.* 1770-1850.

IX.

SONNET.

THIS world is too much with us: late and soon,
  Getting and spending, we lay waste our powers;
Little we see of nature that is ours;
We have given our hearts away,—a sordid boon!
This sea that bares her bosom to the moon,—
The winds that will be howling at all hours,
And are upgathered now like sleeping flowers,—
For this, for everything, we are out of tune;
It moves us not. Great God! I'd rather be
A Pagan, suckled in a creed outworn:
So might I, standing on this pleasant lea,
Have glimpses that would make me less forlorn;
Have sight of Proteus rising from the sea,
Or hear old Triton blow his wreathed horn.

                      —*William Wordsworth.*
                      1770-1850.

X.

A MUSICAL INSTRUMENT.

WHAT was he doing, the great god Pan,
     Down in the reeds by the river?
Spreading ruin and scattering ban,
Splashing and paddling with hoofs of a goat,
And breaking the golden lilies afloat
     With the dragon-fly on the river.

He tore out a reed, the great god Pan,
     From the deep cool bed of the river:
The limpid water turbidly ran,
And the broken lilies a-dying lay,
And the dragon-fly had fled away,
     Ere he brought it out of the river.

High on the shore sat the great god Pan,
     While turbidly flow'd the river;
And hack'd and hew'd as a great god can,
With his hard bleak steel at the patient reed,
Till there was not a sign of a leaf indeed
     To prove it fresh from the river.

He cut it short, did the great god Pan,
     (How tall it stood in the river!)
Then drew the pith, like the heart of a man,
Steadily from the outside ring,
And notch'd the poor dry empty thing
     In holes, as he sat by the river.

"This is the way," laugh'd the great god Pan,
  (Laugh'd while he sat by the river,)
"The only way, since gods began
To make sweet music, they could succeed."
Then, dropping his mouth to a hole in the reed,
  He blew in power by the river.

Sweet, sweet, sweet, O Pan!
  Piercing sweet by the river!
Blinding sweet, O great god Pan!
The sun on the hill forgot to die,
And the lilies reviv'd, and the dragon-fly
  Came back to dream on the river.

Yet half a beast is the great god Pan,
  To laugh as he sits by the river,
Making a poet out of a man:
The true gods sigh for the cost and pain,—
For the reed which grows nevermore again
  As a reed with the reeds in the river.
                    —*Elizabeth Barrett Browning.*
                         1809-1861.

XI.

LIGHT.

THE night has a thousand eyes
　　And the day but one,
Yet the light of the bright world dies
　With the dying sun.

The mind has a thousand eyes,
　　And the heart but one;
Yet the light of a whole life dies
　When love is done.

*　　　　　—Francis William Bourdillon.*
1852 ——

XII.

TO A WATERFOWL.

WHITHER, 'midst falling dew,
    While glow the heavens with the last steps
      of day,
Far, through their rosy depths, dost thou pursue
    Thy solitary way?

    Vainly the fowler's eye
Might mark thy distant flight to do thee wrong,
As, darkly seen against the distant sky,
    Thy figure floats along.

    Seek'st thou the plashy brink
Of weedy lake, or marge of river wide,
Or where the rocking billows rise and sink
    On the chafed ocean-side?

    There is a Power whose care
Teaches thy way along that pathless coast—
The desert and illimitable air—
    Lone wandering, but not lost.

    All day thy wings have fanned,
At that far height, the cold, thin atmosphere,
Yet stoop not, weary, to the welcome land,
    Though the dark night is near.

And soon that toil shall end;
Soon shalt thou find a summer home, and rest,
And scream among thy fellows; reeds shall bend,
    Soon, o'er thy sheltered nest.

    Thou'rt gone, the abyss of heaven
Hath swallowed up thy form; yet, on my heart
Deeply has sunk the lesson thou hast given,
    And shall not soon depart.

    He who, from zone to zone,
Guides through the boundless sky thy certain flight,
In the long way that I must tread alone,
    Will lead my steps aright.
                            —*William Cullen Bryant.*
                                    1794-1878.

XIII.

THE THREE FISHERS.

THREE fishers went sailing out into the West,
  Out into the West as the sun went down;
Each thought of the woman who loved him the best;
  And the children stood watching them out of the
    town;
For men must work, and women must weep,
And there's little to earn, and many to keep,
    Though the harbor bar be moaning.

Three wives sat up in the light-house tower,
  And they trimm'd the lamps as the sun went down;
They look'd at the squall, and they look'd at the
    shower
  And the night rack came rolling up ragged and
    brown!
But men must work, and women must weep,
Though storms be sudden, and waters deep,
    And the harbor bar be moaning.

Three corpses lay out on the shining sands,
  In the morning gleam as the tide went down,
And the women are weeping and wringing their hands
  For those who will never come back to the town;
For men must work, and women must weep,
And the sooner it's over, the sooner to sleep—
    And good by to the bar and its moaning.
                              —*Charles Kingsley.*
                                1819-1875.

XIV

LEAD, KINDLY LIGHT.

LEAD, Kindly Light, amid the encircling gloom,
    Lead Thou me on!
The night is dark, and I am far from nome—
    Lead Thou me on!
Keep Thou my feet; I do not ask to see
The distant scene,—one step enough for me.

I was not ever thus, nor pray'd that Thou
    Shouldst lead me on.
I lov'd to choose and see my path; but now
    Lead thou me on!
I lov'd the garish day and, spite of fears,
Pride rul'd my will: remember not past years.

So long Thy power hath biess'd me, sure it still
    Will lead me on,
O'er moor and fen, o'er crag and torrent, till
    The night is gone;
And with the morn those angel faces smile
Which I have lov'd long since. and lost awhile.
           —John Henry Newman.
           1801-1890.

XV

ISRAFEL.

IN Heaven a spirit doth dwell
    "Whose heart-strings are a lute;"
None sing so wildly well
As the angel Israfel,
And the giddy stars (so legends tell),
Ceasing their hymns, attend the spell
Of his voice, all mute.

Tottering above
In her highest noon,
The enamoured moon
Blushes with love,
While, to listen, the red levin
(With the rapid Pleiads, even,
Which were seven)
Pauses in Heaven.

And they say (the starry choir
And the other listening things)
That Israfeli's fire
Is owing to that lyre
By which he sits and sings—
The trembling living wire
Of those unusual strings.

But the skies that angel trod,
Where deep thoughts are a duty—
Where Love's a grown-up God—
Where the Houri glances are
Imbued with all the beauty
Which we worship in a star.

Therefore, thou art not wrong,
Israfeli, who despisest
An unimpassioned song;
To thee the laurels belong,
Best bard, because the wisest!
Merrily live, and long!

The ecstasies above
With thy burning measures suit—
Thy grief, thy joy, thy hate, thy love,
With the fervor of thy lute—
Well may the stars be mute!

Yes, Heaven is thine; but this
Is a world of sweets and sours;
Our flowers are merely—flowers,
And the shadow of thy perfect bliss
Is the sunshine of ours.

If I could dwell
Where Israfel
Hath dwelt, and he where I,
He might not sing so wildly well
A mortal melody,
While a bolder note than this might swell
From my lyre within the sky.

                              —Edgar Allan Poe.
                                  1811-1849.

XVI.

TEARS, IDLE TEARS.

TEARS, idle tears, I know not what they mean;
    'Tears from the depths of some divine despair
Rise in the heart, and gather to the eyes,
In looking on the happy Autumn-fields,
And thinking of the days that are no more.

Fresh as the first beam glittering on a sail,
That brings our friends up from the underworld,
Sad as the last which reddens over one
That sinks with all we love below the verge;
So sad, so fresh, the days that are no more.

Ah, sad and strange as in dark summer dawns
The earliest pipe of half-awakened birds
To dying ears, when unto dying eyes
The casement slowly grows a glimmering square;
So sad, so strange, the days that are no more.

Dear as remembered kisses after death,
And sweet as those by hopeless fancy feigned
On lips that are for others; deep as love,
Deep as first love, and wild with all regret;
O Death in Life, the days that are no more.
               —Alfred, Lord Tennyson.
                  1809-1892.

XVII.

BREAK, BREAK, BREAK.

BREAK, break, break,
    On thy cold gray stones, O Sea!
And I would that my tongue could utter
    The thoughts that arise in me.

O well for the fisherman's boy,
    That he shouts with his sister at play!
O well for the sailor lad,
    That he sings in his boat on the bay!

And the stately ships go on,
    To the haven under the hill;
But O for the touch of a vanish'd hand,
    And the sound of a voice that is still!

Break, break, break,
    At the foot of thy crags, O Sea!
But the tender grace of a day that is dead
    Will never come back to me.

                        —*Alfred, Lord Tennyson.*
                            1809-1892.

XVIII.

THE BURIAL OF SIR JOHN MOORE.

NOT a drum was heard, not a funeral note,
  As his corse to the rampart we hurried:
Not a soldier discharged his farewell shot
  O'er the grave where our hero we buried.

We buried him darkly at dead of night,
  The sods with our bayonets turning;
By the struggling moonbeam's misty light,
  And the lantern dimly burning.

No useless coffin enclosed his breast,
  Not in sheet or in shroud we wound him;
But he lay like a warrior taking his rest,
  With his martial cloak around him.

Few and short were the prayers we said,
  And we spoke not a word of sorrow,
But we steadfastly gazed on the face of the dead.
  And we bitterly thought of the morrow.

We thought, as we hollowed his narrow bed,
  And smoothed down his lonely pillow,
That the foe and the stranger would tread o'er his
    head,
  And we far away on the billow.

Lightly they'll talk of the spirit that's gone,
  And o'er his cold ashes upbraid him;
But little he'll reck if they let him sleep on
  In the grave where a Briton has laid him.

But half of our heavy task was done,
  When the clock struck the hour for retiring;
And we heard the distant and random gun
  That the foe was sullenly firing.

Slowly and sadly we laid him down
  From the field of his fame fresh and gory;
We carved not a line, we raised not a stone,
  But we left him alone with his glory!

                         —*Charles Wolfe.*
                              1791-1823.

XIX.

A COURT LADY.

HER hair was tawny with gold, her eyes with
    purple were dark,
Her cheeks' pale opal burnt with a red and restless
    spark.

Never was lady of Milan nobler in name and in race;
Never was lady of Italy fairer to see in the face.

Never was lady on earth more true as woman and
    wife,
Larger in judgment and instinct, prouder in manners
    and life.

She stood in the early morning, and said to her
    maidens, "Bring
That silken robe made ready to wear at the court of
    the king.

"Bring me the clasp of diamonds, lucid, clear of the
    mote,
Clasp me the large at the waist, and clasp me the
    small at the throat.

"Diamonds to fasten the hair, and diamonds to fasten
    the sleeves,
Laces to drop from their rays, like a powder of snow
    from the eaves."

Gorgeous she enter'd the sunlight which gather'd her
   up in a flame,
While, straight in her open carriage, she to the hos-
   pital came.

In she went at the door, and gazing from end to end,
"Many and low are the pallets, but each is the place
   of a friend."

Up she pass'd through the wards, and stood at a
   young man's bed:
Bloody the band on his brow, and livid the droop of
   his head.

"Art thou a Lombard, my brother? Happy art thou,"
   she cried,
And smiled like Italy on him: he dream'd in her face
   and died.

Pale was his passing soul, she went on still to a
   second:
He was a grave hard man, whose years by dungeons
   were reckon'd.

Wounds in his body were sore, wounds in his life were
   sorer.
"Art thou a Romagnole?"   Her eyes drove lightnings
   before her.

"Austrian and priest had join'd to double and tighten
   the cord
Able to bind thee, O strong one,—free by the stroke
   of a sword.

"Now be grave for the rest of us, using the life over-
cast
To ripen our wine of the present, (too new,) in glooms
of the past."

Down she stepp'd to a pallet where lay a face like a
girl's,
Young, and pathetic with dying,—a deep black hole
in the curls.

"Art thou from Tuscany, brother? and seest thou,
dreaming in pain,
Thy mother stand in the piazza, searching the list of
the slain?"

Kind as a mother herself, she touch'd his cheeks with
her hands:
"Blessed is she who has borne thee, although she
should weep as she stands."

On she pass'd to a Frenchman, his arm carried off by
a ball:
Kneeling, . . . "O more than my brother! how shall
I thank thee for all?

"Each of the heroes around us, has fought for his
land and line,
But *thou* hast fought for a stranger, in hate of a
wrong not thine.

"Happy are all free peoples, too strong to be dispos-
sess'd:
But blessed are those among nations, who dare to be
strong for the rest!"

Ever she pass'd on her way, and came to a couch
    where pin'd
One with a face from Venetia, white with a hope out
    of mind.

Long she stood and gaz'd, and twice she tried at the
    name,
But two great crystal tears were all that falter'd and
    came.

Only a tear for Venice?—she turn'd as in passion and
    loss,
And stoop'd to his forehead and kiss'd it, as if she
    were kissing the cross.

Faint with that strain of heart she mov'd on then to
    another,
Stern and strong in his death.   "And dost thou suffer,
    my brother?"

Holding his hand in hers:—"Out of the Piedmont
    lion
Cometh the sweetness of freedom! sweetest to live or
    to die on."

Holding his cold rough hands,—"Well, oh, well have
    ye done
In noble, noble Piedmont, who would not be noble
    alone."

Back he fell while she spoke. She rose to her feet
    with a spring,—
"That was a Piedmontese! and this is the Court of
    the King."

                    -Elizabeth Barrett Browning.
                    1809-1861.

XX.

PROSPICE.

FEAR death?—to feel the fog in my throat
    The mist in my face,
When the snows begin, and the blasts denote
    I am nearing the place,
The power of the night, the press of the storm,
    The post of the foe;
Where he stands, the Arch Fear in a visible form,
    Yet the strong man must go;
For the journey is done and the summit attain'd,
    And the barriers fall,
Though a battle's to fight ere the guerdon be gained,
    The reward of it all.
I was ever a fighter, so—one fight more,
    The best and the last!
I would hate that death bandaged my eyes, and for-
    bore,
    And bade me creep past.
No! let me taste the whole of it, fare like my peers,
    The heroes of old,
Bear the brunt, in a minute pay glad life's arrears
    Of pain, darkness and cold.
For sudden the worst turns the best to the brave,
    The black minute's at end,
And the elements' rage, the fiend-voices that rave,
    Shall dwindle, shall blend,
Shall change, shall become first a peace out of pain,
    Then a light, then thy breast,
O thou soul of my soul! I shall clasp thee again,
    And with God be the rest!
                —*Robert Browning.*
                  1812-1890.

XXI.

CONCORD FIGHT.*

BY the rude bridge that arched the flood,
 Their flag to April's breeze unfurled,
Here once the embattled farmers stood,
 And fired the shot heard round the world.

The foe long since in silence slept;
 Alike the conqueror silent sleeps;
And Time the ruined bridge has swept
 Down the dark stream which seaward creeps.

On this green bank, by this soft stream,
 We set to-day a votive stone;
That memory may their deed redeem,
 When, like our sires, our sons are gone.

Spirit, that made those heroes dare
 To die, and leave their children free,
Bid Time and Nature gently spare
 The shaft we raise to them and thee.
                    —*Ralph Waldo Emerson.*
                       1803-1882.

XXII.

ABOU BEN ADHEM.

ABOU BEN ADHEM (may his tribe increase!)
      Awoke one night from a deep dream of peace,
And saw, within the moonlight of his room,
Making it rich and like a lily in bloom,
An angel writing in a book of gold;
Exceeding peace had made Ben Adhem bold,
And to the presence in the room he said,
"What writest thou?" The vision raised its head,
And, with a look made all of sweet accord,
Answered, "The names of those who love the Lord."
"And is mine one?" said Abou. "Nay, not so,"
Replied the angel. Abou spake more low,
But cheerily still; and said, "I pray thee, then,
Write me as one that loves his fellow-men."
The angel wrote, and vanished. The next night
It came again with a great wakening light,
And showed the names whom love of God had blessed,
And lo! Ben Adhem's name led all the rest.

                              —*Leigh Hunt.*
                              1784-1859.

XXIII.

NIGHT.

SWIFTLY walk over the Western wave,
    Spirit of Night!
Out of the misty Eastern cave,
Where, all the long and lone daylight,
Thou wovest dreams of joy and fear,
Which make thee terrible and dear;
    Swift be thy flight!

Wrap thy form in a mantle gray,
    Star inwrought!
Blind with thine hair the eyes of Day!
Kiss him until he be wearied out;
Then wander o'er city and sea and land,
Touching all with thine opiate wand!
    Come, long sought!

When I arose and saw the dawn,
    I sighed for thee;
When light rode high, and dew was gone,
And noon lay heavy on flower and tree;
And the weary Day turned to his rest,
Lingering like an unloved guest
    I sighed for thee.

Thy brother Death came, and cried,
    "Wouldst thou me?"
Thy sweet child, Sleep, the filmy-eyed,
Murmur'd like a noon-tide bee—

"Shall I nestle by thy side?
Wouldst thou me?" And I replied—
      No! not thee.

Death will come when thou art dead,
        Soon, too soon!
Sleep will come when thou art fled;
Of neither would I ask the boon
I ask of thee, beloved Night!
Swift be thine approaching flight!
        Come soon, soon!

                    —*Percy Bysshe Shelley.*
                        1792-1822.

XXIV.

NIGHT AND DEATH.

MYSTERIOUS Night, when our first parent knew
    Thee, from divine report, and heard thy name,
Did he not tremble for this lovely Frame,
This glorious canopy of Light and Blue?
Yet 'neath a curtain of translucent dew,
    Bathed in the ray of the great setting Flame,
    Hesperus with the Host of Heaven, came.
And lo! Creation widened on Man's view.
Who could have thought such darkness lay concealed
    Within thy beams, O Sun! or who could find
Whilst flower, and leaf, and insect stood revealed,
    That to such countless Orbs thou mad'st us blind!
Why do we then shun Death with anxious strife?
If Light can thus deceive wherefore not Life?

                —*Joseph Blanco White.*
                1773-1840.

XXV.

DAFFODILS.

I WANDERED lonely as a cloud
　　That floats on high o'er vale and hills,
When all at once I saw a crowd,
　A host of golden daffodils,
Beside the lake, beneath the trees,
Fluttering and dancing in the breeze.

Continuous as the stars that shine
　And twinkle on the milky way,
They stretched in never-ending line
　Along the margin of a bay;
Ten thousand saw I at a glance
Tossing their heads in sprightly dance.

The waves beside them danced, but they
　Outdid the sparkling waves in glee—
A Poet could not but be gay
　In such a jocund company!
I gazed—and gazed—but little thought
What wealth the show to me had brought;

For oft, when on my couch I lie
　In vacant or in pensive mood,
They flash upon that inward eye
　Which is the bliss of solitude;
And then my heart with pleasure fills,
And dances with the daffodils.
　　　　　　—*William Wordsworth.*
　　　　　　1770-1850.

NINETEENTH CENTURY POEMS.

***

MATTHEW ARNOLD—1822-1888.
      Dover Beach.
      Requiescat.
      Shakespeare.
      Cadmus and Harmonia.
THOMAS BAILEY ALDRICH—1836 ——
      Two Songs from the Persian.
      Identity.
      Nocturne.
MRS. CECIL FRANCIS ALEXANDER—182—
      The Burial of Moses.
WILLIAM BLAKE—1757-1728.
      The Tiger.
ROBERT SEYMOUR BRIDGES—1844 ——
      "My Song Be Like an Air."
ELIZABETH BARRETT BROWNING — 1809-1861.
      A Valediction.
      Crowned and Buried.
ROBERT BROWNING—1812-1889.
      Meeting at Night.
      Evelyn Hope.
      Summum Bonum.
      Echetlos.
      Instans Tyrannus.
      A Toccata of Galuppi's.
      Home Thoughts from Abroad.
      My Star.
      My Last Duchess.
      How They Brought the Good News from Ghent to Aix.

RALPH WALDO EMERSON—1803-1882.
        The Rhodora.
        Brahma.
        Each and All.
        Days.
EUGENE FIELD—1850-1895.
        The Rockaby Lady.
JAMES T. FIELDS—1816-1881.
        The First Appearance at the Odeon.
W. S. GILBERT—1836 ——
        The Nancy Brig.
ARCHIBALD GORDON—
        Grenada—A Song of Exile.
HOMER GREENE—1853 ——
        What My Lover Said.
FITZ-GREENE HALLECK—1790-1867.
        On the Death of Joseph Rodman Drake.
BRET HARTE—1839 ——
        The Heathen Chinee.
        The Mountain Heartsease.
JOHN HAY—1838 ——
        The Lorelei (translation).
        Little Breeches.
FELICIA D. HEMANS—1794-1835.
        Casabianca.
JAMES HOGG—1722-1835.
        The Skylark.
OLIVER WENDELL HOLMES—1809-1894.
        The Last Leaf.
THOMAS HOOD—1799-1845.
        Ruth.
        "I Remember, I Remember."
        The Bridge of Sighs.
        The Death Bed.
LEIGH HUNT—1784-1859.
        Jenny Kissed Me.
JEAN INGELOW—about 1830.
        Exultation (Songs of Seven).
JOHN KEATS—1795-1821.
        Ode to a Nightingale.
        La Belle Dame Sans Merci.
        "Bright Star, Would I Were Steadfast as
            Thou Art."
        Drear-Nighted December.

GUY H. McMASTER—1829-1887.
    Carmen Bellicosum.
GEORGE MEREDITH—1828 ——
    Lucifer in Starlight.
ALICE MEYNELL—
    Renouncement.
F. B. MONEY-COUTTS—
    The Dawn.
THOMAS MOORE—1779-1852.
    Love's Young Dream.
    Oft in the Stilly Night.
    The Bird Let Loose.
WILLIAM MORRIS—1834-1897.
    From the Upland to the Sea.
COVENTRY PATMORE—1823 ——
    The Toys.
EDGAR A. POE—1811-1849.
    Eulalie.
    The Raven.
    Annabel Lee.
ADELAIDE A. PROCTOR—1825-1864.
    The Lost Chord.
    Expectation.
A. T. QUILLER-COUCH—1863 ——
    The Marine.
JAMES WHITCOMB RILEY—1853 ——
    When She Comes Home.
CHRISTINA GEORGINA ROSSETTI—1830-1894.
    Fluttered Wings.
    Old and New Year Ditties.
    The World.
DANTE GABRIEL ROSSETTI—1828-1882.
    A Superscription.
    The Blessed Damosel.
    The Cloud Confines.
    Mary's Girlhood.
C. D. G. ROBERTS—1860 ——
    The Isles.
SIR WALTER SCOTT—1771-1832.
    Lochinvar.
    "Soldier, Rest! thy Warfare O'er."
    A Weary Lot is Thine.
    Pibroch of Donuil Dhu.

BENJAMIN F. TAYLOR—1819-1887.
    The Isles of Long Ago.
WILLIAM M. THACKERAY—1811-1863.
    The Age of Wisdom.
CHARLES TENNYSON TURNER—1808-1879.
    Letty's Globe (Sonnet).
THEODORE WATTS—1836 ——
    The First Kiss.
WILLIAM WATSON—1858 ——
    England to Ireland.
    The First Skylark of Spring.
    Cromwell.
JOHN G. WHITTIER—1807-1892.
    Barbara Frietchie.
    Ichabod.
    Two Angels.
    Skipper Ireson's Ride.
    Telling the Bees.
ELIZABETH WHITTIER—1815-1864.
    Charity.
MRS. A. D. T. WHITNEY—1824 ——
    Behind the Mask.
WALT WHITMAN—1819-1892.
    To the Man of War Bird.
OSCAR WILDE—1856 ——
    Requiescat.
WILLIAM WORDSWORTH—1770-1850.
    Westminster Bridge.
    "Three Years She Grew."
    To a Skylark.
    "Scorn Not the Sonnet."
    Milton (Sonnet).
    London (Sonnet).

A SELECTION FROM
FLEMING H. REVELL COMPANY'S
CATALOGUE.

THREE EXQUISITE BOOKS

The beauty of thought and expression which surrounds Mr. Black's ideal of friendship has encouraged the publishers to complete the harmony by executing the work in the daintiest of styles. As a gift book it cannot be surpassed in appropriateness of sentiment or beauty of production.

Friendship. By Rev. Hugh Black, M. A. With an appreciative note by W. Robertson Nicoll, D. D., and marginal and other decorations by F. Berkeley Smith. Printed in two colors. 12mo, decorated cloth, gilt top, boxed, $1.25.

CONTENTS:

The Miracle of Friendship.
The Culture of Friendship.
The Fruits of Friendship.
The Choice of Friendship.
The Eclipse of Friendship.
The Wreck of Friendship.
The Renewing of Friendship.
The Limits of Friendship.
The Higher Friendship.

Dr. Robertson Nicoll says: "Mr. Hugh Black, who is now, we suppose, the most popular preacher in Scotland, has published a wise and charming little book on Friendship. It is full of good things winningly expressed; and though very simply written, is the result of real thought and experience. Mr. Black's is the art that conceals art.

The Master's Blesseds: The Christ's Secret of Happiness. A Devotional Study of the Beatitudes. By J. R. Miller, D. D. Decorated margins, 16mo, cloth, $1.00.

The peculiar adaptability of the Beatitudes to treatment in a devotional and expository manner, and Dr. Miller's great popularity as a writer of works of this nature were a happy combination, which has resulted in a choice addition to devotional literature. In its mechanical details—deckle-edged paper, ample margins with artistic illuminations, ornamental chapter headings and title page, decorated covers—the book is worthy of subject and author.

The Shepherd Psalm. By Rev. F. B. Meyer, B. A. *Northfield presentation edition,* with illustrations on every page, by Mary A. Lathbury. 12mo, cloth covers, in ink and gold, gilt top, $1.25; full gilt, $1.50.

"Pleasant to the eye and good for food. Mr. Meyer is at his best in this exposition. He leads us in the green pastures and beside the still waters. The illustrations surround and mingle with the text, are printed in light olive green, and combine with paper, type, and presswork to make the book what it is mechanically, an exquisite gem. May this treasury of spiritual comfort be widely circulated."—*The New York Observer.*

THE QUIET HOUR SERIES

This is an age of condensation—ambitious and aggressive folk are even seeking concrete presentations of vital themes. The aim of this series is to supply just such books. A glance at subjects and authors is sufficient to convince one of the importance and value of these dainty little volumes,

Each bound in ivory buckram, stamped on front and reverse cover, 18mo, 25c.

How the Inner Light Failed. A Study of the Atrophy of the Spiritual Sense. To which is added "How the Inner Light Grows." By Newell Dwight Hillis, author of "A Man's Value to Society," "The Investment of Influence," etc., etc.

The Man Who Wanted to Help. By Rev. J.G.K. McClure, D. D., Pres. Lake Forest University.

Young Men in History. By Rev. F. W. Gunsaulus, D. D.

St. Paul; An Autobiography.

Faith Building. By Rev. Wm. P. Merrill, D. D.

The Dearest Psalm and the Model Prayer. By Henry Ostrom, D. D.

The Life Beyond. By Mrs. Alfred Gatty. Adapted by M. A. T.

Mountain Tops with Jesus. By Rev. Theodore L. Cuyler, D. D.

A Life for a Life, and other Addresses. By Henry Drummond. With tribute by D. L. Moody, and portrait.

Peace, Perfect Peace. By Rev. F. B. Meyer, B.A. For the sorrowing.

Money: Thoughts for God's Stewards. By Rev. Andrew Murray.

Jesus Himself. By Rev. Andrew Murray.

Love Made Perfect. By Rev. Andrew Murray.

The Ivory Palaces of the King. By Rev. J. Wilbur Chapman, D. D.

Christ Reflected in Creation. By D. C. McMillan

THE LOOKING UPWARD BOOKLETS

Each with a distinct message of its own, calculated to inspire the reader to higher things. Exceedingly chaste bindings lend an additional charm.

Illustrated, 12mo, decorated boards, each, 30c.

Agatha's Unknown Way. By "Pansy." A story of missionary guidance.

The Dream of Youth. By Hugh Black. M. A., author of "Friendship."

The Spirit Guest. By Josephine Rand. The Story of a Dream.

The Young Man of Yesterday. By Judge A. W. Tenney.

Did the Pardon Come Too Late? By Mrs. Ballington Booth.

Comfort Pease and Her Gold Ring. By Mary E. Wilkins.

My Little Boy Blue. By Rosa Nouchette Carey.

A Wastrel Redeemed. By David Lyall.

A Day's Time Table. By E. S. Elliott, author of "Expectation Corner," etc.

Brother Lawrence; or, The Practice of the Presence of God.

The Swiss Guide. By Rev. C. H. Parkhurst, D.D.

Where Kitty Found Her Soul. By Mrs. J. H. Walworth.

One of the Sweet Old Chapters. By Rose Porter.

The Baritone's Parish. By Rev. J. M. Ludlow,

Child Culture. By Hannah Whitall Smith.

Risen With Christ. By Rev. A. J. Gordon, D. D.

Reliques of the Christ. By Rev. Denis Wortman.

Eric's Good News. By author of "Probable Sons."

Ye Nexte Thynge. By Eleanor A. Sutphen.

Business. By Amos R. Wells.

LITTLE BOOKS FOR LIFE'S GUIDANCE.

"The Revell Co., always quick to see what the religious public will appreciate, is now bringing out a series entitled Little Books for Life's Guidance, which retail at fifty cents each. They are compact in form and prettily bound, each volume containing perhaps 150 pages. Certain characteristics are common to them all. They are written for Christians, and not for worldly people. They are from men whose minds are saturated with the language and thought of the Scriptures. . . . But the main object of all these writers is to develop and make effective a life of faith and devotion. They start with the presupposition, which cannot be gainsaid, that most Christians fall short of those heights on which God expects them to live.—*Congregationalist.*

Long 16mo., decorated cloth, each, 50c.

The Lord's Table. A Help to the Right Observance of the Holy Supper. By Rev. Andrew Murray.

Sin and its Conquerors. Dean Farrar.

Discipleship. Rev. G. Campbell Morgan.

Cheer for Life's Pilgrimage. Rev. F. B. Meyer.

The True Vine. Meditations on John xv. 1-16. Rev. Andrew Murray.

Praying in the Holy Ghost. Rev. G. H. C. MacGregor, M. A.

Saved and Kept. Rev. F. B. Meyer.

Ways to Win. Suggestions with Regard to Personal Work for Christians. By Rev. Dyson Hague.

Waiting on God. Rev. Andrew Murray.

Inspired Through Suffering. Rev. D. O. Mears.

Life's Everydayness. Papers for Women. Rose Porter.

When Thou Hast Shut Thy Door. Amos R. Wells.

Foretokens of Immortality. Newell Dwight Hillis.

Yet Speaking. Rev. A. J. Gordon, D. D.

I Believe. Rev. John Henry Barrows.

A Holy Life, and How to Live It. Rev. G. H. C. MacGregor, M. A.

www.ingramcontent.com/pod-product-compliance
Lightning Source LLC
Chambersburg PA
CBHW021542270326
41930CB00008B/1332